Appet

The Ultimate Recipe Book

By

Les Ilagan

Les Ilagan

DISCLAIMER

Content Arcade Publishing and its authors are joined together in their efforts in creating these pages and their publications. Content Arcade Publishing and its authors make no assurance of any kind, stated or implied, with respect to the information provided.

LIMITS OF LIABILITY

Content Arcade Publishing and its authors shall not be held legally responsible in the event of incidental or consequential damages in line with, or arising out of, the supplying of the information presented here.

Table of Contents

Appetizers

Appetizers

INTRODUCTION

Having a good appetizer is always the best way to begin a sumptuous dinner, it whets the appetite and make you ready for the next course.

During cocktail hour, appetizers and a few drinks can set the mood for the rest of the evening. As they can bring life and joy to any party.

This book will help you learn how to make various appetizers that you can serve for any occasion. It contains a wide selection of delectable little morsels, salad, and soup recipes that will give you a taste of different cuisines like Mediterranean, Middle-Eastern, and Asian.

Most of the recipes in this book are very easy to make and would only require a few minutes of your time. The instructions are made simpler so even beginners won't be having any issue in preparing them.

This book is a part of many cookbook series that I am writing, I hope you have fun trying all the recipes in this book.

So now, let's get it started!

Crab And Corn Canapé With Caviar

If you are looking for a tasty and easy seafood appetizer, this is the perfect recipe for you!

Preparation time: 15 minutes
Total time: 15 minutes
Yield: 24 servings

Ingredients

8 oz. cooked crabmeat, shredded
1 cup light mayonnaise
½ cup sweet corn kernels
½ cup carrot, chopped

½ cup celery, chopped
¼ cup shallots, chopped
¼ cup red caviar (salmon roe)
24 shortbread cookies
salt and freshly ground black pepper

Method

1.   Combine the crabmeat, mayonnaise, sweet corn, carrot, celery, and shallots in a medium bowl. Season with salt and pepper to taste. Mix well.

2.   Spread the prepared crab and corn mixture on each shortbread cookie and top with caviar. Garnish with celery leaves, if desired. Place in a serving dish.

3.   Serve and enjoy.

Beet Pesto Canapé With Shaved Parmesan

A wonderful canapé recipe that is bursting with flavor from the beet root pesto, parmesan, and basil.

Preparation time: 20minutes
Total time: 20 minutes
Yield: 20 servings

Ingredients

2 medium roasted red beets, cut into small pieces
3 cloves garlic, minced

½ cup dry roasted walnuts
½ cup olive oil
2 tablespoons lemon juice
1 tablespoon pine nuts, toasted
½ cup parmesan cheese, grated
20 pcs. shortbread cookies
¼ cup sweet basil, coarsely chopped
salt and freshly ground black pepper

Method

1.   Combine the roasted beets, garlic, walnuts, lemon juice, and pine nuts in a food processor. Pulse 2-3 times until it forms a coarse paste. With the motor on, gradually add the oil, until the mixture is thickened and smooth. Season with salt and pepper, to taste.

2.   Spread the prepared beet pesto on each shortbread cookie and top with shaved parmesan. Garnish with basil. Place in a serving dish.

3.   Serve and enjoy.

Feta Cherry Tomato And Olive Canapé

These Mediterranean mini skewers are totally delicious!

Preparation Time:10minutes
Total Time:10 minutes
Yield:24 servings

Ingredients
2 cups cherry tomatoes, halved
8 oz. feta cheese, diced
24 black olives, pitted
24 decorative skewers or toothpicks

Method

1.   Thread olives, cherry tomatoes, and feta cheese onto the skewers or toothpicks. Place in a serving dish.

2.   Serve and enjoy.

Cheddar And Green Grape Skewers

This appetizer recipe combines the sweet-tangy taste of grapes and the saltiness of cheddar cheese.

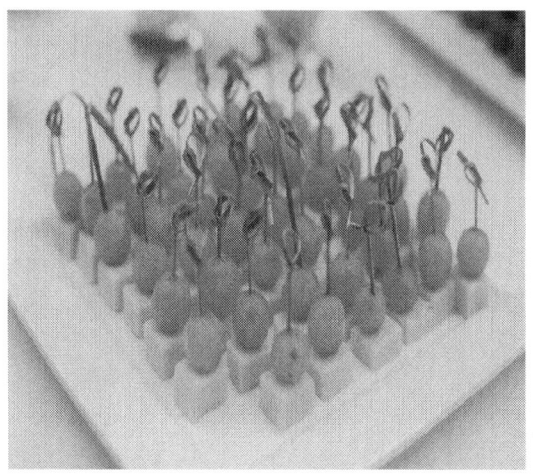

Preparation time: 10minutes
Total Time: 10 minutes
Yield: 20 servings

Ingredients

8 oz. cheddar cheese
20 seedless grapes

20 decorative small skewers or toothpicks

Method

1. Cut the cheddar cheese into small cubes.

2. Thread the cheese and grapes onto skewers or toothpicks. Place in a serving dish.

3. Serve and enjoy.

Radish Sour Cream and Herb Canapé

A nice looking and delicious appetizer recipe made with radish, sour cream, and chives!

Preparation time: 15 minutes
Total time: 15 minutes
Yield: 8 servings

Ingredients

4 radishes, thinly sliced
1 cup sour cream
¼ cup fresh chives, chopped
¼ teaspoon garlic powder

4 slices wholegrain bread
freshly ground black pepper

Method

1.   Cut the bread slices diagonally to make 2 triangles.

2.   Combine the sour cream, chives, and garlic powder in a small bowl. Season with pepper, to taste. Mix well.

3.   Spoon 2 tablespoons of sour cream mixture and spread onto the bread slices. Garnish with chopped chives. Place in a serving dish.

4.   Serve and enjoy.

Fresh Tomato Bruschetta with Herb

This delightful bruschetta with fresh vegetables and herb is can be done in a snap!

Preparation time: 15 minutes
Total time: 15 minutes
Yield: 8 servings

Ingredients

1 French bread
3 medium tomatoes, chopped
1 large white onion, chopped
1 celery stalk, chopped

1 clove garlic, minced
2 tablespoons olive oil
2 tablespoons lemon juice
2 tablespoons fresh parsley, chopped
salt and freshly ground black pepper

Method

1.   Cut the French bread horizontally to make 8 equal slices. Toast bread slices in a toaster oven.

2.   Combine the tomatoes, onion, celery, garlic, olive oil, lemon juice, and parsley in a medium bowl. Toss to coat and mix well. Season with salt and pepper, to taste.

3.   Top each bread toast with the tomato mixture. Place in a serving dish.

4.   Serve immediately and enjoy.

Guacamole Canapé With Corn Tortilla Chips

This Mexican-inspired appetizer is packed with awesome flavors and nutrition.

Preparation Time:15 minutes
Total Time:15minutes
Yield:16 servings

Ingredients

Guacamole:
1 medium ripe avocado, mashed
1 medium tomato, finely chopped
1 medium onion, finely chopped
½ medium lemon, juiced
2 tablespoons fresh coriander leaves, finely chopped

2 cloves garlic, finely chopped
¼ teaspoon paprika
¼ teaspoon cumin, ground
salt and freshly ground black pepper
corn tortilla chips, to serve

Method

1.   Combine avocado, tomato, onion, lemon juice, coriander, garlic, paprika, and cumin in a medium bowl. Season with salt and pepper, to taste. Transfer in a serving dish.

2.   Serve guacamole with corn tortilla chips on the side.

3.   Enjoy.

Chicken Vienna Sausage Bites

If you are looking for a quick, easy, and tasty appetizer, this is the perfect recipe for you!

Preparation time: 10minutes
Total time: 10 minutes
Yield: 24servings

Ingredients

24 chicken Vienna sausage

¾ cup ketchup

1 tablespoon pickle relish

1 teaspoon honey

½ teaspoon Worcestershire sauce

¼ teaspoon wholegrain mustard
freshly ground black pepper
toothpicks, to serve

Method

1.   Combine ketchup, pickle relish,

honey, Worcestershire sauce, and

mustard in a small bowl. Season with

pepper to taste.

2.   Insert 1 toothpick in the middle

of each Vienna sausage. Arrange them in a

serving platter and serve with prepared

dipping sauce.

3.   Enjoy.

Bruschetta with Tomato Mozzarella and Herb

This is a delicious and healthy appetizer recipe, a sure hit!

Preparation time:8 minutes
Total time:15 minutes
Yield:12 servings

Ingredients

¼ cup olive oil
¼ teaspoon garlic powder
¼ teaspoon freshly ground black pepper
12 thin slices of French bread

24 cherry tomato, chopped
8oz. mozzarella cheese, shredded
24 fresh basil leaves, chopped

Method

1.   Mix together the olive oil, garlic powder and pepper in a small bowl. Brush each bread slice with olive oil mixture. Cook in a toaster oven until golden.

2.   Top each bread slice with tomatoes, mozzarella, and basil. Return into the toaster oven and cook for another 3 minutes or until the cheese melts.

3.   Place in a serving dish**.**

4.   Serve and enjoy.

Easy Italian Bruschetta

This Italian-inspired appetizer recipe with cherry tomatoes, capers, and mushrooms are so delicious and filling.

Preparation time: 15minutes
Total time: 15minutes
Yield:12servings

Ingredients

2 tablespoons balsamic vinegar
2 tablespoons olive oil
2 tablespoons fresh parsley, chopped
½ teaspoon Italian seasoning

24 cherry tomatoes, thinly sliced
2 tablespoons capers, drained
1 shallot, minced
½ cup button mushrooms, thinly sliced
12 thin slices of toasted French bread

Method

1.   Combine together balsamic vinegar, olive oil, parsley, and Italian seasoning in a medium bowl. Mix well.

2.   Add the tomatoes, capers, shallot, and mushrooms. Toss to coat. Season with salt and pepper, to taste.

3.   Top each toast with tomato mixture.

4.   Place in a serving dish.

5.   Serve and enjoy.

Salmon Canapé with Goat Cheese and Dill

This delightful appetizer also makes a great party snack!

Preparation time: 15 minutes
Total time: 15 minutes
Yield: 12 servings

Ingredients

12 oz. smoked salmon, thinly sliced
6 oz. goat cheese
2 oz. light mayonnaise

1 shallot, minced
1 clove garlic, minced
1 tablespoon lemon juice
1 tablespoon fresh mixed herbs, chopped
12 thin slices of French bread, toasted
salt and freshly ground black pepper
fresh dill weed, for garnish

Method

1.   Combine the goat cheese, mayonnaise, shallot, garlic, lemon juice, and herbs in a small bowl. Season with salt and pepper, to taste.

2.   Top each bread toast with goat cheese mixture and a slice of salmon. Garnish with fresh dill. Place in a serving dish.

3.   Serve immediately and enjoy.

Shrimp and Cream Cheese on Cucumber Cups

Serve this cucumber cups with shrimp and cream cheese for an appetizer and your guests will surely be delighted!

Preparation time: 20minutes
Total time: 20 minutes
Yield: 16 servings

Ingredients
4small cucumbers
16 medium cooked shrimps, peeled and deveined
2 tablespoons olive oil
1 tablespoon lime juice

½ teaspoon dried parsley
6 oz. cream cheese
¼ cup light mayonnaise
1 clove garlic, minced
½ teaspoon coriander seed, ground
salt and freshly ground black pepper

Method

1.   Using a knife or peeler, score the length of each cucumber alternately. Trim the ends and cut crosswise to make 4 pieces. Scoop out the seeds, leaving some at the bottom to hold the filling. Set aside.

2.   In a medium bowl, mix together olive oil, lime juice, and parsley. Add the shrimps and toss to coat. Season with salt and pepper, to taste. Let sit for a few minutes.

3.   Meanwhile, combine the cream cheese, mayonnaise, garlic, and coriander in a small bowl. Season with salt and

pepper, to taste. Mix well. Transfer into a piping bag with star tip.

4.   Pipe the cream cheese filling onto the center of each cucumber cup. Top individually with shrimp. Place in a serving dish.

5.   Serve and enjoy.

Spiced Egg Salad Canapé

This appetizer recipe is also perfect for a quick breakfast or snack.

Preparation time:15 minutes
Total time:15 minutes
Yield:16servings

Ingredients

8slices whole wheat bread
¾ cup light mayonnaise
3 large eggs, chopped
½ cup scallions, chopped
1 tablespoon Dijon mustard

½ teaspoon paprika
¼ teaspoon garlic powder
¼ teaspoon lemon pepper

Method

1. Cut each bread slice in half (horizontally), to make 16 slices. Set aside.

2. Combine together the mayonnaise, eggs, scallions, mustard, paprika, garlic powder, and lemon pepper in a small bowl. Mix thoroughly.

3. Top each bread slice with egg mixture. Place in a serving dish.

4. Serve and enjoy.

Easy Salmon Yogurt and Herb Canapé

This easy to prepare canapé with salmon and herb makes a fantastic meal starter or snack.

Preparation time:15 minutes
Total time:15 minutes
Yield:10 servings

Ingredients

1 French baguette

10 (1 oz.) slices smoked salmon

3/4 cup Greek yogurt

2 tablespoons fresh chives, finely chopped

½ teaspoon cumin, ground

salt and freshly ground black pepper
chopped fresh dill weed, for garnish

Method

1. Cut the baguette into 10 thin equal slices. Set aside.

2. Combine together the yogurt and fresh chives in a small bowl. Season with salt and pepper, to taste. Mix well.

3. Top each bread slice with 1 tablespoon yogurt mixture and 1 slice salmon. Garnish with dill and sprinkle with cumin. Place in a serving dish.

4. Serve and enjoy.

Pita Crisps with Tzatziki Dip

This appetizer recipe doesn't only taste great but nutritious too!

Preparation time: 15 minutes
Total time: 15 minutes
Yield: 8 servings

Ingredients

1 cup Greek yogurt

1 small cucumber, chopped

2 tablespoons lemon juice

2 tablespoons green onion, chopped

½ teaspoon sweet paprika

salt and freshly ground black pepper
pita crisps, to serve

Method

1.	Combine yogurt, cucumber, lemon juice, green onion, and paprika in a small bowl. Season with salt and pepper, to taste.

2.	Arrange pita crisps in a serving platter and serve with prepared Tzatziki dip.

3.	Serve and enjoy.

Quick and Easy Devilled Eggs

Start your meal with a bite of these awesome devilled eggs!

Preparation Time: 15 minutes
Total Time: 15 minutes
Yield: 10 servings

Ingredients

5 hard-boiled eggs
3/4 cup mayonnaise
2 tablespoons Dijon mustard
1 tablespoon pickle relish
½ teaspoon wholegrain mustard
½ teaspoon cumin, ground
½ teaspoon coriander seed, ground
½ teaspoon cayenne pepper

salt and freshly ground black pepper
1 teaspoon paprika, to serve
thinly sliced black olives, for garnish
thinly sliced red bell pepper, for garnish

Method

1.	Remove and discard the shells from the eggs. Cut in half lengthwise.

2.	Scoop out the egg yolks and put them in a medium bowl.

3.	Add the mayonnaise, Dijon mustard, pickle relish, cumin, coriander, and cayenne pepper. Season with salt and pepper, to taste. Mix well. Transfer into a piping bag with star tip.

4.	Pipe egg mixture onto the hollow part of the egg white halves. Sprinkle with cumin.

5.	Place in a serving dish. Sprinkle with paprika. Garnish with olives and red bell pepper.

6.	Serve and enjoy.

Crunchy Garlic Bread with Herb

This crunchy garlic bread recipe is not only good for accompaniment for pasta but can also be served as an appetizer.

Preparation time:10 minutes
Total time:30 minutes
Yield: 8 servings

Ingredients

1 French baguette
½ cup olive oil
1 tablespoon garlic, minced

1 tablespoon fresh parsley, minced
1 tablespoon fresh basil, minced
salt and freshly ground black pepper

Method

1. Preheat the oven to 425 F.

2. Cut the baguette horizontally to make 8 slices.

3. Combine olive oil, garlic, parsley, and basil in a small bowl. Season with salt and pepper to taste.

4. Brush each bread slice with oil mixture. Place in a baking sheet.

5. Bake in the oven for 10-15 minutes or until golden brown. Leave inside the oven for another 5 minutes.

6. Serve in a serving platter and enjoy.

Oven-Baked Mozzarella Sticks with Herbs

These awesome mozzarella sticks are very easy to make and absolutely delicious. Serve with marinara sauce or any kind of dipping sauce.

Preparation Time:30minutes
Total Time:30 minutes
Yield:16 servings

Ingredients
1 pound mozzarella cheese
1 cup bread crumbs
½ teaspoon garlic powder
½ teaspoon dried oregano
½ teaspoon dried parsley
3 egg whites, lightly beaten

2 tablespoons milk
cooking oil spray
freshly ground black pepper

Method

1.   Preheat the oven to 425 F.

2.   Cut the mozzarella into 16 (3-inch) pieces.

3.   Mix together the breadcrumbs, garlic powder, oregano, and parsley in a medium bowl.

4.   In a small bowl, combine the milk and egg whites. Season with pepper.

5.   Dip the mozzarella sticks onto the egg whites then coat all sides with breadcrumb mixture.

6.   Arrange them to make a single layer in a baking pan or cookie sheet. Spray with oil.

7.   Bake in the oven for 20-25 minutes or until golden brown. Cool slightly.

8.   Place in a serving platter and serve with your favorite dipping sauce.

9.   Enjoy.

Crunchy Chicken Fingers

This delicious chicken finger recipe is can be eaten as an appetizer or snack.

Preparation Time:30minutes
Total Time:30 minutes
Yield:8 servings (3-4 pcs. per serving)

Ingredients
2 pounds chicken breast, boneless and skinless
1 cup bread crumbs
½ teaspoon garlic powder
1 teaspoon dried rosemary
1/3 cup buttermilk
2 egg whites

cooking oil spray
salt and freshly ground black pepper
choice of dipping sauce, to serve

Method

1.   Preheat the oven to 425 F.

2.   Cut the chicken breast fillet into 3-inch strips.

3.   Combine the breadcrumbs, garlic powder, and rosemary in a medium bowl.

4.   In a small bowl, combine the butter milk and egg whites. Season with salt and pepper.

5.   Dip the chicken onto the buttermilk mixture then coat all sides with breadcrumb mixture.

6.   Arrange them to make a single layer in a baking sheet. Spray with oil.

7.   Bake in the oven for 20-25 minutes or until golden brown. Cool slightly.

8.   Place in a serving platter and serve with your favorite dipping sauce.

9.   Enjoy.

Homemade Dinner Prawn Cocktail

This is a very popular appetizer at dinner cocktails, where prawns are normally served with spicy dip in cocktail glasses.

Preparation time: 10 minutes
Total time: 10 minutes
Yield: 8 servings

Ingredients
2 pounds boiled prawns, peeled (tails intact)
¾ cup ketchup

2 tablespoons lemon juice
1/2 teaspoon garlic, minced
1/2 teaspoon chili powder
1/4 teaspoon sweet paprika
1/4 teaspoon cumin, ground
2 tablespoons olive oil
1/2 teaspoon dried sage
salt and freshly ground black pepper
fresh parsley, for garnish
8 cocktail glasses

Method

1.   Combine the ketchup, lemon juice, garlic, chili powder, paprika, and cumin, in a small bowl. Mix well.

2.   Place the prawns in a shallow bowl and drizzle with olive oil. Season with salt and pepper, to taste. Sprinkle with sage.

3.   Transfer prawns in a serving platter and serve with prepared spicy dip.

4.   Enjoy.

Mini Caprese Salad Skewers

A Mediterranean-inspired recipe that is perfect to start any meal.

Preparation time:15 minutes
Total time:15 minutes
Yield:16 servings

Ingredients

¼ cup balsamic vinegar
2 tablespoons extra-virgin olive oil
1 tablespoon Dijon mustard
salt and freshly ground black pepper

16 mozzarella balls
16 cherry tomato halves
16 fresh basil leaves
16toothpicks or decorative skewers

Method

1.   Whisk together the balsamic vinegar, oil, and Dijon mustard in a small bowl. Season with salt and pepper, to taste.

2.   Thread the cherry tomato, mozzarella ball, and basil onto each toothpick or skewer.

3.   Place the caprese skewers in a serving dish. Drizzle with balsamic vinaigrette.

4.   Serve immediately and enjoy.

Tortilla Chips with Salsa Supreme

This Mexican-inspired appetizer recipe will surely become everyone's favorite!

Preparation time:15 minutes
Total time:15 minutes
Yield:12 servings

Ingredients

2 tablespoons olive oil
2 tablespoons lime juice
¼ teaspoon cumin, ground
¼ teaspoon paprika
¼ teaspoon coriander seed, ground

4 medium tomatoes, finely chopped
1 medium onion, chopped
2cloves garlic, minced
1 jalapeno pepper, chopped
1 tablespoon cilantro, chopped
2 tablespoons sour cream
¼ cup scallions or chives, chopped
¼ cup olives, pitted and sliced
salt and freshly ground black pepper
2 packs tortilla corn chips

Method

1.   In a medium bowl, whisk together the olive oil, lime juice, cumin, paprika, and coriander.

2.   Add the tomatoes, onion, garlic, jalapeno, and cilantro. Season with salt and pepper, to taste. Toss to combine well. Place in a serving bowl. Top with sour cream.

3.   Serve tortilla chips in a platter with salsa at the center. Sprinkle with scallions and olives.

4.   Enjoy.

Tuna Onion and Dill Canapé

This yummy canapé recipe with tuna, onion, and dill is can be made in a flash!

Preparation time: 10 minutes
Total time:10 minutes
Yield:24 servings

Ingredients

24thin slices of toasted French bread
1 cup canned tuna in water, drained and flaked
¾ cup light mayonnaise
1 medium white onion, finely chopped

1 tablespoon fresh dill weed, finely chopped
1 tablespoon pickle relish
salt and freshly ground black pepper
more fresh dill weed, for garnish

Method

1.   Combine the tuna, light mayonnaise, onion, dill, and pickle relish in a medium bowl. Season with salt and pepper, to taste.

2.   Spread 1 tablespoon tuna mixture onto each toasted bread slice. Garnish with fresh dill weed.

3.   Place in a serving dish. Serve and enjoy.

Cheesy Pesto Canapé

This appetizer recipe has the perfect blend of flavors from the pesto sauce and cheddar cheese.

Preparation time: 15 minutes
Total time: 15 minutes
Yield: 8servings

Ingredients

8thin slices of French bread
1/2 cup pesto sauce
1/3 cup cheddar cheese, grated
freshly ground black pepper

Method

1.   Spread 1 tablespoon pesto sauce onto each bread slice. Season with pepper to taste. Sprinkle with cheddar cheese.

2.   Toast in a toaster oven for 3-5 minutes or until golden brown.

3.   Enjoy.

Cheddar Tomato and Basil Canapé

This is a quick and easy canapé recipe that can be enjoyed as an appetizer or snack.

Preparation time:15 minutes
Total time:15 minutes
Yield:24 servings

Ingredients

24shortbread cookies
24 (1/8-inch) slice of American cheese
12 cherry tomatoes
24 fresh basil leaves

Method

1. Cut the cherry tomatoes in half (crosswise).
2. Top each cookie with 1 slice of cheese, cherry tomato, and basil.
3. Place in a serving dish.
4. Serve and enjoy.

Tuna and Cucumber Canapés

These wonderful mini tuna wraps are great for appetizer, snacks, or lunch!

Preparation time: 15 minutes
Total time: 15 minutes
Yield: 12 servings (3 pieces per serving)

Ingredients
2/3 canned tuna in water, drained and flaked
1/2 cup light mayonnaise
1 shallot, finely chopped
1/4 teaspoon dried thyme

1/4 teaspoon coriander seed, ground
1 medium cucumber, thinly sliced
6 Romaine lettuce leaves
3 large pita bread, toasted and warmed
salt and freshly ground black pepper
fresh parsley, for garnish

Method

1.   Combine the tuna, mayonnaise, shallot, thyme, and coriander in a medium bowl. Season with salt and pepper, to taste.
2.   Divide lettuce leaves and cucumber slices among 3 pita breads. Top with tuna mixture. Roll it up to enclose the filling. Cut each wrap into four equal portions to make four rolls.
3.   Place in a serving dish. Garnish with fresh parsley.
4.   Serve and enjoy.

Spiced Meatball Appetizer with Blue Cheese

Your guests will surely be delighted with these amazing little meatballs!

Preparation time: 20 minutes
Total time: 20 minutes
Yield: 6 servings

Ingredients

1 pound beef sirloin, ground
½ cup breadcrumbs
1 medium egg, lightly beaten

4 oz. blue cheese
2 tablespoons fresh basil
½ teaspoon cayenne pepper
¼ teaspoon paprika
freshly ground black pepper
vegetable oil, for frying
toothpicks or decorative mini skewers
dipping sauce, to serve

Method

1. In a mixing bowl, combine ground beef, breadcrumbs, egg, blue cheese, basil, cayenne pepper, and paprika. Season with pepper to taste. Mix well.

2. Scoop 1 teaspoon from the beef mixture and form into balls. Repeat with the remaining mixture.

3. Heat oil in a non-stick pan over medium-high heat. Cook the meatballs until browned. Transfer to a plate lined with paper towels and allow to drain excess oil.

4. Insert toothpick onto each meatball

and serve with your favourite dipping sauce.

5. Enjoy.

Mini Kiwi and Cheese Skewers

This mini fruit and cheese kebab recipe is so delicious and healthy too.

Preparation time: 15 minutes
Total time: 15 minutes
Yield: 12 servings

Ingredients

4 medium kiwifruit, peeled
4 oz. cheddar cheese
4 oz. mozzarella cheese

toothpicks or decorative mini skewers

Method

1. Cut the kiwi, cheddar, and mozzarella cheese into small squares.
2. Thread the kiwi alternately with the cheese onto each toothpick or skewer.
3. Place in a serving dish.
4. Serve and enjoy.

Marinated Garlic Shrimps on Skewers

If you love seafood, try this quick, garlicky, and delicious shrimp skewers!

Preparation time:15 minutes
Total time:15 minutes
Yield:4 servings (2 skewers each)

Ingredients

2 pounds fresh shrimp, peeled and deveined (tails intact)
¼ cup olive oil
2 tablespoons lemon juice
1 tablespoon Dijon mustard

½ teaspoon garlic powder
2 tablespoons toasted garlic
salt and freshly ground black pepper
chopped fresh dill weed, for garnish
wooden skewers

Method

1.   Combine olive oil, lemon juice, and garlic powder in a non-reactive shallow bowl. Add the shrimps. Toss to coat. Let sit for at least 30 minutes.

2.   Preheat grill to high.

3.   Thread the shrimps onto the skewers. Grill for about 7-8 minutes turning once. Transfer to a serving dish. Sprinkle with toasted garlic and fresh dill weed.

4.   Serve and enjoy.

Curried Chicken Balls with Coriander

Simple yet flavorful appetizer recipe that everyone will surely love.

Preparation time: 10 minutes
Total Time: 20 minutes
Yield: 6 servings

Ingredients

1 pound chicken breast fillet, ground
½ cup breadcrumbs
1 medium egg, lightly beaten
1 medium onion, chopped

2 tablespoons fresh coriander leaves, chopped
1 teaspoon curry powder
salt and freshly ground black pepper
vegetable oil, for frying
toothpicks or decorative mini skewers
dipping sauce, to serve

Method

1.   Mix together the ground chicken, breadcrumbs, egg, onion, coriander, and curry powder. Season with salt and pepper, to taste.

2.   Scoop 1 teaspoon from the chicken mixture and form into balls. Repeat with the remaining mixture.

3.   Heat oil in a non-stick pan over medium-high heat. Fry the chicken balls until browned. Transfer to a plate lined with paper towels and allow to drain excess oil.

4.   Insert toothpick onto each chicken ball and serve with your favorite dipping sauce.

5.   Enjoy.

Cheese and Olive Canapé

This could be the easiest and fastest appetizer that you can prepare, not to mention that it only calls for 2 very basic ingredients – olives and cheese.

Preparation time: 5 minutes
Total time: 5 minutes
Yield: 16 servings

Ingredients

8 oz. cheddar cheese or mozzarella cheese
16 green olives, pitted
16 toothpicks or decorative skewers

Method

1.   Cut the cheddar or mozzarella cheese into 16 (1-inch) cubes.

2.   Thread 1 cheese and 1 olive onto each toothpick or skewer. Place in a serving dish.

3.   Serve and enjoy.

Easy Homemade Tuna Stuffed Peppers

This super delicious appetizer recipe will definitely make a statement at your next party!

Preparation time:10 minutes
Total time:40 minutes
Yield:4 servings

Ingredients

1 cup canned tuna, flaked
1 large onion, chopped
1 medium egg
½ cup breadcrumbs

½ cup cottage cheese

2 tablespoons tomato sauce

2 tablespoons fresh parsley, chopped

¼ teaspoon cumin, ground

¼ teaspoon paprika

4 medium red bell pepper

Method

1.   Preheat your oven to 425 F.

2.   Combine the tuna, onion, egg, breadcrumbs, cottage cheese, tomato sauce, parsley, cumin, and paprika in a medium bowl. Season with pepper to taste. Mix well.

3.   Cut the tops of the bell pepper and scoop out the seed and core from the hole.

4.   Stuff each bell pepper with tuna mixture. Bake in the oven for about 25 minutes.

5.   Place in a serving platter.

6.   Serve and enjoy.

Spicy Shrimp Appetizer with Herbs

This spicy shrimp dish with herbs is can be served either as an appetizer or main.

Preparation time:15 minutes
Total time:15 minutes
Yield:4 servings

Ingredients

2 tablespoons unsalted butter
1 teaspoon garlic, minced
1 pound shrimps, peeled and deveined
1 medium red bell pepper, thinly sliced

2 tablespoons lemon juice
½ teaspoon chili powder
½ teaspoon paprika
½ cup green onions, chopped
2 tablespoons fresh dill weed, chopped
salt and freshly ground black pepper

Method

1. Melt butter in a skillet over medium heat. Stir-fry garlic until fragrant and golden, about 1-2 minutes.

2. Add the shrimps, bell pepper, lemon juice, chili powder, and paprika. Cook for 5-7 minutes, stirring often. Season with salt and pepper to taste.

3. Transfer to a serving dish and sprinkle with green onions and dill.

4. Serve and enjoy.

Hot Buffalo Wings

This homemade Buffalo wings recipe is really spicy but you can cut back on hot pepper sauce if you think you are not up for it.

Preparation time:5 minutes
Total time:15 minutes
Yield:8 servings

Ingredients

2 pounds deep fried chicken wings, separated at joints

3/4 cup hot pepper sauce

1/3 cup unsalted butter

1 1/2 tablespoons vinegar

1 teaspoon Worcestershire sauce
1/2 teaspoon cayenne pepper
1/2 teaspoon garlic powder
1/4 teaspoon coriander seed, ground
salt and freshly ground black pepper to
taste

Method

1.   In a medium saucepan, combine the hot pepper sauce, butter, vinegar, Worcestershire sauce, cayenne pepper, garlic powder, and coriander. Bring to a simmer over medium heat, stirring constantly.

2.   Add the fried chicken wings onto the saucepan stir to coat well. Cook further 1-2 minutes. Season with salt and pepper to taste.

3.   Transfer in a serving dish and serve immediately.

Hummus with Pita Crisps

*Try this fantastic hummus recipe served with
pita crisps for appetizer or snack.*

Preparation time: 15 minutes
Total time: 15 minutes
Yield: 16 servings

Ingredients
2 cups canned chickpeas, drained
(reserve half of the liquid)
3 cloves garlic (minced)
2 tablespoons tahini
¼ cup lemon juice

1 tablespoon lemon zest (finely grated)
salt and freshly ground black pepper
2 tablespoons olive oil
1 teaspoon paprika
pita crisps, cut into small triangles

Method

1. Place the chickpeas, garlic, tahini, lemon juice, zest, and the reserved liquid from chickpeas in a food processor. Process until smooth. Season with salt and pepper, to taste.

2. Transfer into a serving bowl. Drizzle with olive oil. Sprinkle with paprika.

3. Arrange the pita crisps in a serving platter and serve with prepared hummus on the side.

4. Enjoy.

Mini Chicken Ham and Pineapple Skewers

This simple appetizer has a perfect blend of flavors from the chicken ham and pineapple chunks.

Preparation time:10 minutes
Total time:10 minutes
Yield:16 servings

Ingredients

16 chicken ham, thinly sliced
16 pineapple chunks
16 toothpicks or decorative skewers

Method

1. Thread a chunk of pineapple and a slice of chicken ham on each skewer.

2. Place in a serving dish.

3. Serve and enjoy.

Beet and Rocket Salad with Gorgonzola

This salad is so easy to make, refreshing, and absolutely delicious!

Preparation time: 10 minutes
Total time: 10 minutes
Yield: 4 servings

Ingredients

1/2 cup extra-virgin olive oil
1/2 cup frozen orange juice concentrate
1/4 cup balsamic vinegar
4 medium beets, scrubbed and trimmed

6 cups baby rocket leaves
1/2 cup Gorgonzola cheese, crumbled
1/3 cup chopped walnuts
salt and freshly ground black pepper

Method

1.　　Mix together olive oil, orange juice concentrate, and balsamic vinegar in a salad bowl.

2.　　Add the beets, rocket leaves, and Gorgonzola cheese. Toss to combine. Season with salt and pepper to taste.

3.　　Transfer to individual plates and sprinkle with chopped walnuts.

4.　　Serve and enjoy.

Marinated Cucumber and Onion Salad

This easy, tasty, and healthy cucumber salad is the perfect meal starter if you are watching your weight because it is low in calories.

Preparation time:10 minutes
Total time:1 hour 10 minutes
Yield:4servings

Ingredients

¼ cup balsamic vinegar
¼ cup extra-virgin olive oil

1 clove garlic, minced
2 medium cucumbers
1 medium red onion, thinly sliced
salt and freshly ground black pepper

Method

1.   Cut the cucumber into 1/8-inch thick slices. Set aside.

2.   Mix together balsamic vinegar, olive oil, and garlic in a salad bowl.

3.   Add the cucumbers and onion slices. Toss to coat. Season with salt and pepper to taste. Cover and refrigerate for at least an hour to absorb flavors.

4.   Transfer to serving dish.

5.   Serve and enjoy.

Arugula Salad with Mozzarella and Pomegranates

Start your meal with this scrumptious and nutritious fresh arugula salad recipe with mozzarella, pomegranates and pecans.

Preparation time: 10 minutes
Total time: 10 minutes
Yield: 4 servings

Ingredients

2 cups cherry tomatoes, halved

6 cups baby rocket leaves
6 oz. mozzarella balls
1/3 cup pomegranate seeds
1/3 cup pecan nuts
salt and freshly ground black pepper
choice of dressing, to serve

Method

1. In a salad bowl, combine cherry tomatoes, rocket leaves, mozzarella balls, pomegranates, and pecans. Toss to combine. Season with salt and pepper to taste.

2. Divide salad among 4 individual plates and drizzle with your choice of dressing.

3. Serve and enjoy.

Quick and Easy Caprese Salad

Caprese Salad is a very popular dish in Italy that highlights 3 main ingredients namely – tomato, mozzarella cheese and fresh basil. This is great for appetizer, snack, or a quick lunch.

Preparation time: 10 minutes
Total time: 10 minutes
Yield:4 servings

Ingredients

2 cups cherry tomatoes, halved
8 oz. mozzarella balls

2 cups sweet basil leaves
½ cup balsamic vinegar
¼ cup olive oil
salt and freshly ground black pepper

Method

1. In a salad bowl, combine cherry tomatoes, mozzarella balls, and fresh basil. Toss to combine. Season with salt and pepper to taste.

2. Divide salad among 4 individual plates and drizzle with balsamic vinegar and olive oil.

3. Serve and enjoy.

Vegetarian Salad Greek-Style

This awesome Greek-style salad recipe makes a fantastic meal starter.

Preparation time:10 minutes
Total time:10 minutes
Yield:4 servings

Ingredients

2 medium tomatoes, sliced
1 medium red onion, thinly sliced
1 cup feta cheese, cut into small cubes
½ cup black olives, pitted

1 head iceberg lettuce, leaves separated and torn
Red Wine Vinaigrette Dressing:
½ cup olive oil
¼ cup red wine vinegar
2 teaspoon Dijon mustard
¼ teaspoon dried oregano
¼ teaspoon onion powder
salt and freshly ground black pepper

Method

1.   Whisk together olive oil, red wine vinegar, Dijon mustard, oregano, and onion powder in a small glass bowl. Set aside.

2.   Place the tomatoes, red onion, feta cheese, black olives, and lettuce in a large salad bowl. Toss to combine. Season with salt and pepper, to taste.

3.   Divide salad among 4 individual plates. Drizzle with prepared red wine vinaigrette.

4.   Serve and enjoy.

Strawberry Spinach and Goat Cheese Salad

This fresh summer salad recipe with spinach, strawberries, and goat cheese is a sure winner!

Preparation time:10 minutes
Total time:10 minutes
Yield:4 servings

Ingredients

6 cups baby spinach
1 cup goat cheese, crumbled
1 cup strawberries, sliced

Lemon-Herb Vinaigrette:
½ cup extra-virgin olive oil
2 Tbsp. lemon juice
2 tsp. Dijon mustard
¼ tsp. dried parsley
salt and black pepper, to taste

Method

1.   In a small bowl, whisk together olive oil, lemon juice, Dijon mustard, and dried parsley.
2.   Combine the spinach, goat cheese, and strawberries in a salad bowl. Toss to combine. Season with salt and pepper, to taste.
3.   Divide salad in individual plates. Drizzle with prepared lemon-herb vinaigrette.
4.   Serve and enjoy.

Fresh Beet Cucumber and Tomato Salad

This delightful salad recipe with beets, cucumber, and grape tomatoes complements well with the creamy yogurt dressing.

Preparation Time:10 minutes
Total Time:10 minutes
Yield:4 servings

Ingredients

2 medium beets, thinly sliced
2 medium cucumber, thinly sliced
1 cup grape tomatoes, halved
1 large red onion, thinly sliced

Creamy Yogurt Dressing with Dill:
6 oz. Greek yogurt
1 shallot, finely chopped
1 tablespoon lemon juice
1 tablespoon fresh dill weed, chopped
salt and freshly ground black pepper

Method

1.   Combine yogurt, shallot, lemon juice, and dill in a small bowl. Season with salt and pepper, to taste. Mix well.

2.   Toss beets, cucumber, tomatoes, and red onion in a large salad bowl.

3.   Transfer and divide the salad mixture in individual salad plates.

4.   Serve with prepared yogurt dressing and enjoy.

Garden Fresh Salad with Ranch Dressing

This salad recipe will give you a refreshing feeling in every bite. A great way to start dinner!

Preparation time:10 minutes
Total time:10 minutes
Yield:4 servings

Ingredients

1 head iceberg lettuce, torn into small pieces
1 medium cucumber, thinly sliced
2 cups cherry tomatoes, halved

½ cup olives, pitted

Easy Homemade Ranch Dressing:
1/4 cup sour cream
1/4cup buttermilk
1 tablespoon fresh chives, finely chopped
1 tablespoon fresh parsley, finely chopped
¼ teaspoon Worcestershire sauce
¼ teaspoon garlic powder
¼ teaspoon cayenne pepper

Method

1.   Combine sour cream, buttermilk, chives, parsley, Worcestershire sauce, garlic powder, and cayenne pepper in a small bowl. Mix well.

2.   Toss the lettuce, cucumber, cherry tomatoes, and olives in a large salad bowl.

3.   Divide the salad mixture in individual salad plates.

4.   Serve salad with prepared ranch dressing on the side and enjoy.

Classic Herbed Tomato Soup

A traditional soup recipe made with tomatoes and herbs that will comfort you to the soul.

Preparation time:10 minutes
Total time:50 minutes
Yield:4 servings

Ingredients

2 tablespoons butter

¼ cup scallions, chopped

1 (29 ounce) can diced tomatoes

2 cups chicken broth, unsalted

1 tablespoon white sugar
½ teaspoon dried parsley
2 cups half and half cream
salt and freshly ground black pepper

Method

1.   Melt butter in a medium saucepan or stockpot over medium heat. Stir-fry scallions for 1-2 minutes.

2.   Add the tomatoes, chicken broth, sugar, and parsley. Cook for 30 minutes.

3.   Add the half and half cream and simmer for another 5 minutes, stirring often. Season with salt and pepper to taste.

4.   Transfer soup in a blender or food processor and process until smooth, blend in batches if needed. Return to saucepan and cook for 2 minutes.

5.   Ladle in individual bowls and garnish with fresh parsley.

6.   Serve and enjoy.

Creamed Broccoli and Dill Soup with Croutons

This is a delicious soup recipe that is perfect for any occasion.

Preparation Time:10minutes
Total Time:50 minutes
Yield:4 servings

Ingredients

2 tablespoons butter
2 shallots, chopped
2 cups broccoli florets, coarsely chopped
2 cups chicken broth, unsalted
2 cups half and half cream
1 tablespoon dill weed, chopped

1/4 teaspoon onion powder
1/4 teaspoon garlic powder
salt and freshly ground black pepper
fresh dill weed, for garnish
croutons, for topping

Method

1.   Melt butter in a medium saucepan or stockpot over medium heat. Stir-fry shallots for 1-2 minutes.

2.   Add broccoli, chicken broth, onion powder, and garlic powder. Cook for 30 minutes.

3.   Add the half and half cream and dill. Simmer for another 5 minutes, stirring often. Season with salt and pepper to taste.

4.   Transfer soup in a blender or food processor and process until smooth, blend in batches if needed. Return to saucepan and cook for 2 minutes.

5.   Ladle in individual bowls and top with croutons. Garnish with fresh dill weed.

6.   Serve and enjoy.

Pumpkin Soup with Sour Cream

Fall won't be complete without serving a bowl of this wonderful soup.

Preparation time: 10 minutes
Total time: 40 minutes
Yield: 4 servings

Ingredients

2 tablespoons olive oil, to serve

1 medium onion, chopped

1 teaspoon garlic (minced)

1 celery stalk, chopped

2 cups pumpkin puree

2 cups chicken broth

½ teaspoon cinnamon, ground

¼ teaspoon nutmeg

¼ teaspoon paprika

2/3 cup sour cream

salt and freshly ground black pepper

fresh parsley, for garnish

Method

1.   Heat oil in a medium saucepan or stockpot over medium heat. Stir-fry onion, garlic, and celery for 1-2 minutes.

2.   Add pumpkin puree, chicken broth, cinnamon, nutmeg, and paprika. Cook for 20 minutes, stirring occasionally. Season with salt and pepper to taste.

3.   Ladle in individual bowls and top with a dollop of sour cream. Garnish with fresh parsley.

4.   Serve and enjoy.

Creamed Vegetable Soup with Turmeric

This delicious soup makes a wonderful starter, just serve with some crusty bread.

Preparation time:10 minutes
Total time:50 minutes
Yield:4 servings

Ingredients

2 tablespoons olive oil, to serve
1 medium onion, chopped

1 teaspoon garlic (minced)
1 medium carrots, chopped
2 celery stalks, chopped
2 cups chicken broth
½ teaspoon turmeric powder
½ teaspoon coriander, ground
2 cups half and half cream
salt and freshly ground black pepper
fresh coriander leaves, for garnish

Method

1. Heat oil in a medium saucepan or stockpot over medium heat. Stir-fry onion and garlic for 1-2 minutes.

2. Add the carrot, celery, and chicken broth, turmeric, and coriander. Cook for 30 minutes, stirring occasionally.

3. Stir in half and half cream and cook further 3-5 minutes or until heated through. Season with salt and pepper to taste.

4. Ladle in individual bowls. Garnish with fresh coriander leaves.

5. Serve and enjoy.

Cream of Fresh Asparagus Soup with Parmesan

This is a great tasting appetizer recipe that surely you don't want to miss!

Preparation time: 15 minutes
Total time: 50 minutes
Yield: 4 servings

Ingredients

2 tablespoons olive oil, to serve
1 medium onion, chopped
1 teaspoon garlic (minced)

1 pound asparagus, trimmed and cut into small pieces
2 celery stalks, chopped
2 cups vegetable broth
1 ½ cups milk
1 (6 oz.) Greek yogurt
1 tablespoon lemon juice
¼ cup parmesan, finely grated
salt and freshly ground black pepper

Method

1. Heat oil in a medium saucepan or stockpot over medium heat. Stir-fry onion and garlic for 1-2 minutes.

2. Add the asparagus, celery, and chicken broth. Cook for 30 minutes, stirring occasionally.

3. Transfer soup in a blender. Process until smooth, blend in batches if needed. Return soup in the saucepan.

4. Stir in milk, yogurt, lemon juice, and parmesan cheese. Cook for another 2-3 minutes or until heated through. Season

with salt and pepper to taste.

5. Ladle in individual bowls. Garnish with asparagus tips, if desired.

6. Serve and enjoy.

Printed in Great Britain
by Amazon